Mushrooming with confidence

Alexander Schwab

Alexander Schwab grew up in Switzerland and was awarded a
Masters Degree in philosophy and history at Aberdeen Univer-
sity. His main interests are all aspects of fishing, hunting and
mushrooming. He lives in the beautiful Emmental region of
Switzerland and when not mushrooming, fishing or hunting,
he is thinking or writing about them.

Mushrooming with confidence

Positive identification of the
most delicious common mushrooms

Alexander Schwab

Consultant: Roy Mantle

First published by Merlin Unwin Books Ltd (Ludlow UK) in 2011

Merlin Unwin Books Ltd
Palmers House
7 Corve Street
Ludlow
Shropshire SY8 1DB
UK
www.merlinunwin.co.uk

ISBN 9781 906122 362
Alexander Schwab has asserted his right under the Copyright, Designs and Patents Act 1988 to be identified as the author of this work.

Picture Credits:
The full picture credits of the contributing photographers Frank Moser (www.frank-moser.de), Klaus Bornstedt (www.klaus-bornstedt.de), Hans Bister, Roberto Fernández and Thomas Beer are given on the website www.mushrooming.co.uk

Every effort has been made to ensure the accuracy of the information in this book. In no circumstances can the publisher or the author accept any liability for any loss, injury or damage of any kind resulting from an error in or omission from the information contained in this book. The same applies to the website www.mushrooming.co.uk and its contents and links.

Design and production by Kurt Wüst, Urtenen-Schönbühl, Switzerland
Printed and bound by Star Standard Industries (PTE) Ltd

Contents

Mushrooming
with
confidence

How to use this guide

1. Read the entire book *twice* in order to be sure you understand the approach
2. Study the *Gills, Ridges, Tubes* and *Spines* sections until you're confident you can correctly distinguish these features; then you're ready for a foray
3. Double-check the mushrooms you have picked, back at home, by completing the positive identification checklist, step by step

The mushrooming with confidence method

What does 'edible' mean?

There are few pleasures as exclusive and satisfying as a feast of delicious wild mushrooms. Likewise, there are few pleasures that can be as fraught with anxiety as mushroom hunting. Nothing curbs the appetite more effectively than a nagging worry that what you eat might make you ill – or kill you. Conventional mushroom identification books promise to enable you to identify hundreds, if not thousands, of edible mushrooms. However, 'edible' simply implies 'not poisonous' and is no indicator of culinary value. Cardboard is 'edible' too.

Mushrooming with confidence focuses on the very best and most common mushrooms and allows you to identify them safely. In this book you'll find only the mushrooms of the top league, and luckily these are easily and safely identified provided you follow the method presented here. If you carry out all the instructions to the letter you'll enjoy the most delicious mushrooms, untroubled by fear and doubt.

Learn to leave a mushroom

Some people find it really difficult not to pick everything they spot. It might be

It is tempting to pick every beautiful mushroom one comes across, but indiscriminate mushroom hunting is not only dangerous: it makes a nonsense of conservation.

edible, they think. They're encouraged in this attitude by encyclopaedic mushroom identification books displaying a bewildering multitude of mushrooms. This induces indiscriminate mushroom hunting of the 'pick first, ask questions later' variety, which is the wrong approach. Back home, attempts to identify the edible ones with the help of a conventional mushroom identification book invariably fail because there is not enough detail to be truly confident you have the right species.

Even advanced mushroom pickers often face many uncertainties. The same mushroom looks different at each stage of its development and different again when conditions are, for example, very wet or very dry.

Look–alike poisonous species

Conventional mushroom guides always include warnings against look-alike poisonous species. This simply adds to the uncertainty. *Mushrooming with confidence* asks you not to compare but positively to identify the most valuable mushrooms by their unique and unmistakable features. This approach automatically eliminates dangerous or deadly species, provided you play your part correctly. Basically this means:

1. Be disciplined enough to leave alone most mushrooms you encounter
2. Look closely at what you see in front of you, not at what you wish was there
3. Stick to the rules and tick off every box on the identification page in this book

You wouldn't buy a soggy, worm-infested, half rotten mushroom in the supermarket. So why pick it in the woods? Quality, as seen in this example of perfect charcoal burners, is what the discerning mushroom hunter is after.

Mushrooming with confidence aims to make you - not a mycologist - but an expert on the best edible mushrooms. That in turn might provoke a deeper interest in the world of mushrooms. In either case: enjoy!

The tools of the trade

The minimum equipment required consists of a knife and a basket or linen bag for transportation. Mushrooms want to breathe. If you put them in a plastic bag they'll suffocate in no time at all and your beautiful fresh mushrooms transform into a soggy mess.

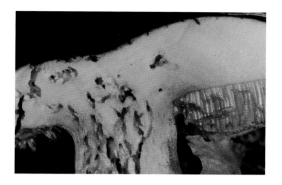

If possible, use a proper mushroom knife with an integrated brush for cleaning. As the first cleaning of the mushroom should be done in the woods, the brush is very useful.

The size of mushrooms

The measurements given in this book are average values. The size of mushrooms can vary disproportionately due to weather conditions: if it is, for example, very dry, the mushrooms will be smaller than average. On the other hand, if conditions are perfect (humidity, ideal substrate) you might come across surprisingly large specimens.

Worm-infested mushrooms

There is no need to discard an otherwise perfect mushroom because of worms. Just cut away the wormy bits. The worm-free pieces are as good as ever – the quality is in no way compromised.

Cutting or pulling?

Cutting mushrooms just above the ground, rather than pulling them up, leaves the mycelium intact. Cutting can actually stimulate the growth of new mushrooms in the mycelium, whereas uprooting can inhibit repeat growth. Sometimes, though, the stem may have features needed for identification, in which case, you will have to pull up a specimen.

Raw mushrooms

Do not eat any wild mushrooms raw as there is a potential risk of catching something nasty from them: some animals (mice, roe deer) or, worse still, dogs, may have left a mark on them, so avoid busy dog-walking routes.

What is a mushroom?

A mushroom is a highly complex organism. Here are the essentials:

Fruitbody

The technical term for what is colloquially called the 'mushroom' is the 'fruitbody'. Mycologically speaking, the real mushroom is the mycelium, which is a fine structure of filaments on or in the forest soil. What we see as mushrooms (the fruitbody) are like the apples on an apple tree.

Cap

The caps of mushrooms have many different forms but what we're interested in is what is under the cap. Under the cap you'll find either...

Gills
Ridges
Tubes or
Spines

Gills, ridges, tubes, and spines produce, contain and release the spores. Wind and rain disperse the spores. Given the right conditions new mycelia and mushrooms form from the spores.

Stem

Mycelium

The mycelium here is visible to the naked eye.

This is a close-up of about 4mm (¹/₄") of the same mycelium as seen under a microscope. When conditions are right, the mycelium forms a fruitbody, pushing the mushroom up in order to disperse the spores or to wait for you to come along and pick it.

Gills, ridges, tubes and spines

Gills, ridges, tubes and spines provide four neat and useful divisions for identification purposes. Most mushrooms fall into one of these four categories. This is the reason why the first step in the identification process is to determine whether you are dealing with gills, tubes, spines or ridges. As the following pages show, this is much easier than it sounds.

Gills

Gills are the radiating blades on the underside of the cap. They fan out in a distinctly regular way. Gills have precise forms and come in many colours. Some of them are brittle, some of them are soft.

They can be rubbed off or separated from the underside of the cap quite easily. Gills are always attached to the stem or the cap in a uniform way.

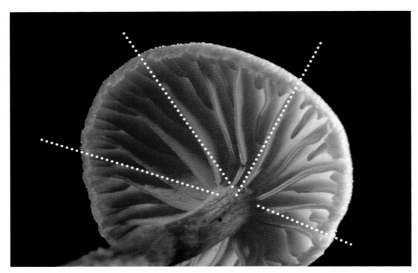

In perfect condition the distinctly regular way in which the gills fan out is clearly visible.

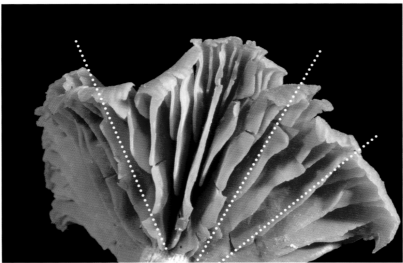

Weather-beaten or old gills might be damaged or broken but on closer inspection their regularity will become apparent. Damage or no damage: either way they look as if drawn with a ruler.

In their regular way, gills differ in spacing and formation.
For example:

Gills can fork
once or more.

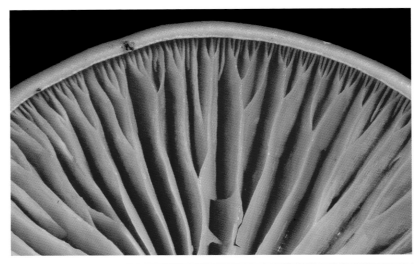

Gills can be
mixed: long and
short gills.

Gills can be crowded.

Gills can be widely spaced.

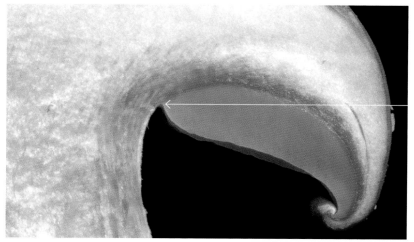

Gills are always uniformly attached to the cap or the stem. They start radiating from the same height along the stem or the same line around the cap.

Ridges

Ridges are on the underside of the cap and form no regular pattern. They have no precise form. They can't easily be rubbed off or separated from the cap or stem.

Ridges are on the underside of the cap. They are not just attached to the cap or stem: they're part of them, which is why you can't rub or pull them off easily.

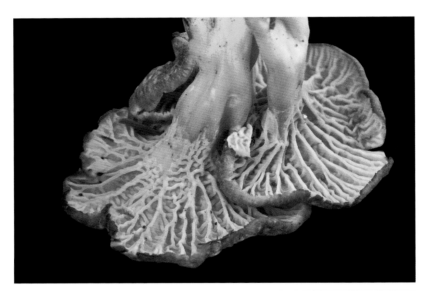

Ridges are cross-veined, irregular and don't form a set, uniform pattern. They are not attached to the stem in a distinct and regular way, as gills are: they are part of the stem.

The ridges are part of the stem. There is no distinct pattern in the way they grow out of the stem. Some ridges begin further up, some further down the stem. There is no regularity.

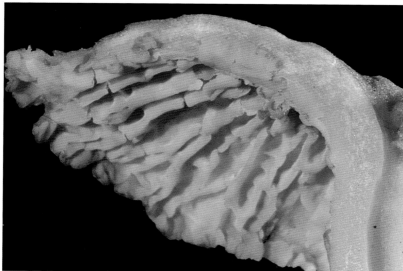

In contrast to gills and tubes, the section of a mushroom with ridges shows no typical features. Because of the irregular nature of ridges each section will look different, whereas with tubes and gills you will find the same features each time.

Gills and ridges in comparison

Gills

Regular, geometric.

Attached to cap or stem.

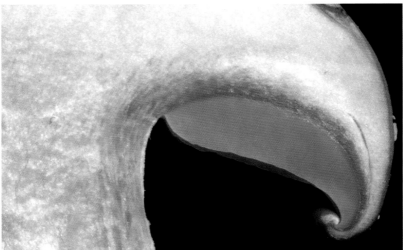

Ridges

Irregular,
cross-veined.

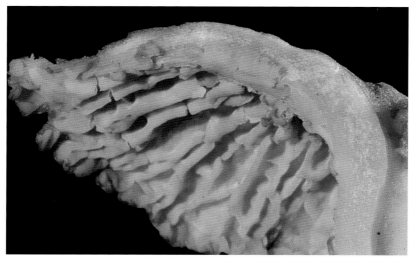

Part of cap
and stem.

Tubes

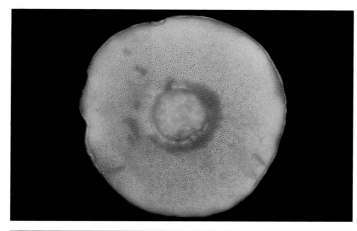

Tubes are fine and tightly packed on the underside of the cap. Without a cross-section only the lower ends of the tubes are visible as little holes which are called pores. The pores have a sponge-like appearance, which is why the underside of mushrooms with tubes is often referred to as 'spongy'. Some tubes are more tightly packed than others; in this case the pores are smaller. Tubes can be removed from the cap easily.

Pores form a regular pattern resembling a sponge.

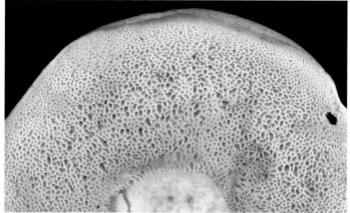

This cross-section shows the tubes and the pores.

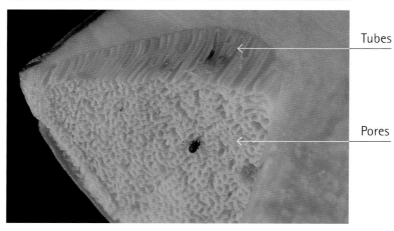

Tubes

Pores

Spines

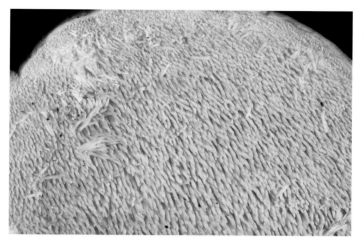

Spines hang like stalactites from the cap.

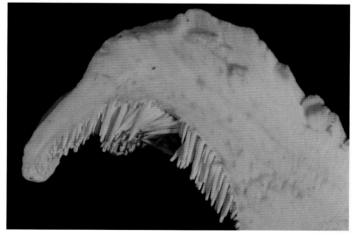

Positively identifying mushrooms

Mushrooms
with gills

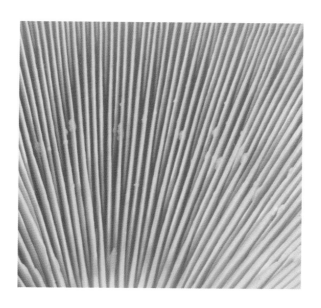

The Field Mushroom

Agaricus campestris var. campestris

The field mushroom is probably the most popular mushroom, not least because it is so common. It grows mainly on pastures and grassland but could appear on any grassy, well-fertilized patch of land, even on the lawn. Its culinary value is undisputed and the flavour of the wild variety is superior to the farmed specimens you can hunt for in the supermarket. If it is a wet and humid summer, start looking for field mushrooms as early as June.

The field mushroom rarely walks alone. It almost always appears in groups or 'fairy rings'. There might be the odd field mushroom somewhere all on its own — leave it.

The cap of the field mushroom is white. The size of the cap ranges from 3 to 8cm (1"–3").

Veil

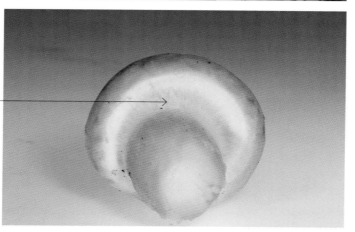

When you find a group or fairy ring of field mushrooms, there will inevitably be specimens at various stages of growth. If the veil is still covering the gills, section the mushroom and ascertain that the gills are pink (see next page).

Veil

The gills of a field mushroom button must not — emphatically not — be white but light pink, and any bruises on the flesh are pink. The pink of the bruises varies in intensity.

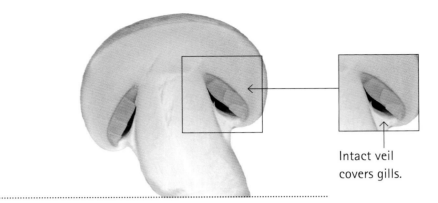

Intact veil covers gills.

Note:
Gills light pink.
Flesh bruises faintly pink.

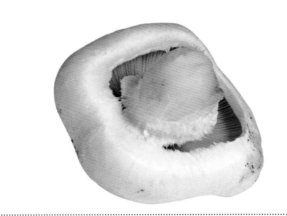

Veil

As the field mushroom grows, the veil is ripped, leaving a small, fragile ring. This will eventually disappear but almost always traces of it remain visible on the stem.

Faint traces of veil must be seen on the stem.

The mature field mushroom: deep pink gills and faint traces of the ring left on the stem. The stem is slightly tapered and must not have a bulb at the base. Stems are straight or lightly bent as on this specimen here.

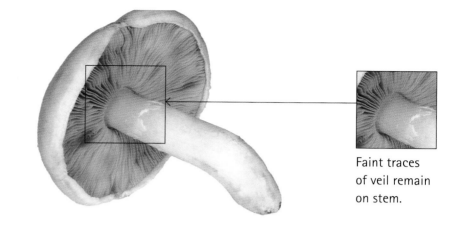

Faint traces of veil remain on stem.

Section of the mature field mushroom: the pink bruising is more intense here and the gills are deep pink. The gills are not attached to the stem.

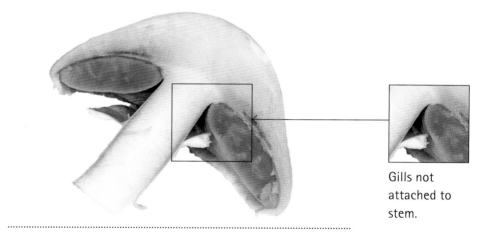

Gills not attached to stem.

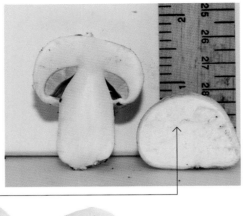

Be extremely careful when collecting button-sized field mushrooms. Always cross-section them and make sure the pink gills are visible. In the picture (left) a baby giant puffball has 'smuggled' itself into the basket. It is harmless but some buttons might be really problematic. Again: the gills must be clearly discernible and pink. Field mushrooms can grow up to 15cm (6") in height.

The gills of the field mushroom at different stages: light pink as in the button and chocolate brown in the late stages of growth. If the gills are dark brown or predominantly black, the field mushroom has lost its culinary value.

Positive ID Checklist

The Field Mushroom

- ☑ Found in groups or fairy ring
- ☑ Not found in woods
- ☑ White cap
- ☑ Stem tapered, no bulb on base
- ☑ Pink to chocolate brown gills
- ☑ Gills not attached to stem
- ☑ Flesh colours pink when bruised
- ☑ Gills must match gill colour bar (above)

Avg. size across cap:	10cm (4")
Season:	June to October
Habitat:	Pastures, meadows, grassland
Tip:	Horse pastures are always very promising
Culinary rating:	10 out of 10

Campestris means 'in the plains'

The Wood Blewit

Lepista nuda

If conditions are right, the wood blewit will show as early as April and May. The normal season for this excellent mushroom is September to November. It is quite common and can be found in coniferous and deciduous forests. Apart from its culinary value, it is said to reduce blood pressure. Some report allergic reactions to wood blewits. The first time you eat it, try only a little. Like all other wild mushrooms, it should not be eaten raw.

Wood blewits are found in groups or fairy rings.

When young, the caps are of an intense mauve with a pronounced purple tinge.

When older, the colours fade. The older specimens get a tan, so to speak.

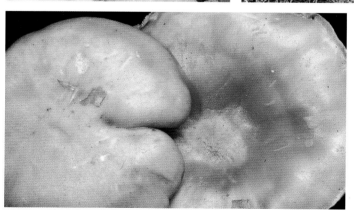

Size of cap
c. 15cm (6").

Size of cap
c. 10cm (4").

Size of cap
c. 5cm (2").

The convex cap of
the young mushroom
flattens out as it
matures.

Just as the intensity
of the cap colour
changes, the gill
colour changes from
a deep purple to a
faint mauvish purple.
The gills must be
mauvish purple and
never brown.

The stem has
vertical streaks
in silvery mauve-
purple and is
slightly fibrous.

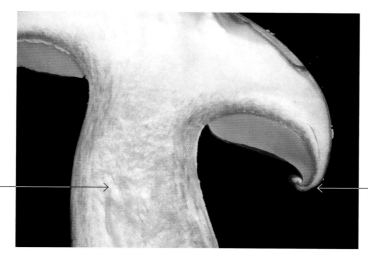

The flesh
must be pale
mauve-purple,
never brown or
yellow-brown.

The margin of
the cap must be
smooth and never
frayed.

Positive ID Checklist
The Wood Blewit

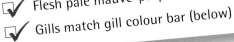

- ☑ Found in the wood
- ☑ Found in groups or fairy ring
- ☑ Cap matches cap colour bar (above)
- ☑ Margin of cap smooth, not frayed
- ☑ Stem vertically streaked
- ☑ Flesh pale mauve-purple
- ☑ Gills match gill colour bar (below)

Avg. size across cap:	10cm (4")
Season:	April, May. Or September, October, November.
Habitat:	Coniferous, deciduous and mixed woods
Tip:	Tends to grow in the same places
Culinary rating:	9 out of 10

Nuda means 'naked'

The Shaggy Ink Cap

Coprinus comatus

Luckily, this distinct and delicious mushroom is quite common. Although single specimens are sometimes found standing alone in the middle of nowhere, it usually appears in masses, especially along waysides but also in the woods. The shaggy ink cap is also called 'the lawyers wig', a name which aids safe identification of a mushroom which is easy to recognize anyway.

The cylindrical cap covered with curly scales is typical of the shaggy ink cap.

The shaggy ink cap grows up to 20cm (8") in height. Do not pick anything you take to be a shaggy ink cap smaller than 5cm (2") in height.

On the left, the perfect specimen for the table. On the right, one that's too far gone.

The stem is hollow. Discard it: it is tough. As long as the gills are white, the shaggy ink cap is fine to eat.

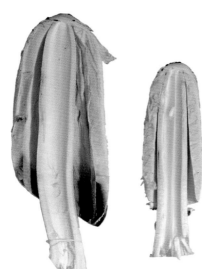

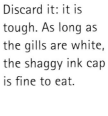

The quick demise of a beautiful mushroom. The gills liquefy, becoming a black inky substance. In these stages the shaggy ink cap is not fit for consumption.

Gill colour bar

Positive ID Checklist

The Shaggy Ink Cap

- ☑️ Found in groups
- ☑️ Cylindrical cap
- ☑️ Curly scales on cap
- ☑️ Hollow stem
- ☑️ Minimum height 5cm (2")
- ☑️ Gills match gill colour bar (above)

Avg. height fit for consumption:	10cm (4")
Season:	March to October
Habitat:	Woods, grassland, parks, wayside verges
Tip:	Do not store or transport for a long time. The quality deteriorates by the hour.
Culinary rating:	9 out of 10

Comatus means 'shaggy'

The Parasol

Macrolepiota procera

Picking small specimens of the parasol isn't entirely safe because the identifiable features are not fully visible. Besides, you get less mushroom, the specimen on the left is the ideal parasol from the culinary and safety point of view. Parasols show mostly in groups or fairy rings. Where there is one there is usually another.

These are fine specimens and make an excellent meal.

The general colour is brownish cream to white. The paler the mushroom the more distinctive the snakeskin pattern on the stem.

The cap can measure up to 35cm (14") across.

It's all about size: they push up to 40cm (16") in height.

The gills are off-white to cream and do not change colour when touched or bruised. The gills are attached to the cap, not to the stem.

The ring on the stem is white on top and brown underneath and can be slid up and down easily.

The snakeskin pattern on the stem below the ring is typical for the parasol mushroom.

The stem is hollow (right) and forms a mycelium-covered bulb at the base (far right). The bulb is an integral part of the stem. The stem is fibrous and no good for eating. Discard, or dry and crush with pestle and mortar for a fine mushroom powder for seasoning.

Stem and bulb must be one smooth piece.

Positive ID Checklist

The Parasol

☑ Over 15cm (6") in height

☑ Gills do not bruise

☑ Gills attached to cap, not to stem

☑ Snakeskin pattern on stem

☑ Movable ring

☑ Hollow, fibrous stem

☑ Bulb integral part of stem

☑ Gills must match gill colour bar (above)

Avg. height ideal for consumption:	20cm (8")
Season:	July to October
Habitat:	Wood clearings, edges of woods, wayside verges
Tip:	Batter and deep-fry the cap for a special treat
Culinary value:	9 out of 10

Procera means 'tall'

The Shaggy Parasol

Chlorophyllum rhacodes

Only collect the shaggy parasol in deciduous or coniferous woods. Some people can get a tummy upset (allergic reaction) from the shaggy parasol, so only eat it in small amounts first. Most people are fine with it, as with all the mushrooms in this book. But a small quantity to start with is always a good idea, as with any new food.

Shaggy cap, hence the name shaggy parasol. That, however, is not its key identifying feature.

The gills are off-white to cream and bruise red. The gills are attached to the cap, not the stem. The flesh of the cap also bruises red.

The stem is hollow and bruises red.

The stem forms a bulb which is covered by mycelium. The bulb is a smooth, integral part of the stem.

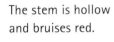

The intensity of the red bruising varies and also fades after the initial cutting.

The stalk is whitish, smooth and shows no particular pattern. The ring is two-tiered and easily movable.

Positive ID Checklist

The Shaggy Parasol

- ✓ Minimum height to pick: 10cm (4")
- ✓ Gills off-white and bruise red
- ✓ Gills attached to cap, not to stem
- ✓ Ring on stem movable
- ✓ Hollow stem which bruises red
- ✓ Bulb smooth and part of stem
- ✓ Red bruise matches bruise colour bar (above)

Avg. size across cap:	10–15cm (4"–6")
Season:	August to October
Habitat:	Deciduous and coniferous woods
Tip:	Do not pick in gardens or parks
Culinary rating:	9 out of 10

Rhacodes means 'ragged' or 'tattered'

The Oyster Mushroom

Pleurotus ostreatus

Apart from the fresh air, the reward for braving the frosty winter weather for a woodland walk could be the oyster mushroom. Oyster mushrooms need the frost to fructify (except a species from Florida). They grow wild on tree trunks, but, since they can easily be farmed commercially, they are often found in supermarkets. The name reflects the fact that the structure of the oyster mushroom resembles oyster banks. Just as fresh oysters are a delicacy, so are fresh oyster mushrooms, and like oysters they should be consumed as soon as possible after harvesting. Opinions differ as to the oyster mushroom's suitability for freezing or drying. There is no difference of opinion, however, about which of the various species of oyster mushrooms is best: from a culinary angle, the oyster mushroom portrayed here (*pleurotus ostreatus*) is the only true oyster mushroom.

Tree trunks, stumps and logs are the places to look for the oyster mushroom. The common beech is probably the best bet but oyster mushrooms can also be found on other deciduous trees.

Clusters of oyster mushroom viewed from the side, from the front and from below. The fan-shaped caps overlap in tiers. The gills are white or off-white. The oyster bank structure is the key identifying feature.

The stems are usually short and stubby and often fused together. They are tough: discard them.

The gills are white to off-white and run down the stem — if there is a distinct stem at all.

The gills turn brownish when old. At this stage, the oyster mushroom is no longer fit for consumption. But there is always next year ...

Cap size usually between 5cm (2") and 20cm (8") but in exceptional cases can be up to 40cm (16"). From the culinary point of view, the smaller cap sizes are preferable because the bigger the cap, the less tasty it is. The cap is smooth, without a veil or traces of a veil (see page 35).

The cap colours of oyster mushrooms vary considerably and look livelier before cutting. The intensity of the colours fades as they dry.

Dove grey-blue

Green-grey

Grey-brown

Slate grey

Positive ID Checklist

The Oyster Mushroom

- ✓ Oyster bank structure
- ✓ Fan-shaped caps
- ✓ No veil or traces of veil
- ✓ Gills correspond to gill colour bar (above)

Avg. size cap:	5–20cm (2"–8")
Season:	November to March
Habitat:	Tree trunks, stumps, logs of deciduous trees
Tip:	Grows year after year in the same place
Culinary rating:	9 out of 10

Ostreatus means 'oyster'

The St George's Mushroom

Calocybe gambosa

This mushroom appears around St. George's Day (April 23). Around that time, morels are still going strong but the dedicated morel hunter won't be distracted by the appearance of this mushroom. It has a distinct mealy smell which some experts describe as 'pleasant and strong' while others find it rather off-putting. That mealy smell is one of the key identifying features. Those who go for the St. George's mushroom claim that it is best sliced and fried in butter. It also dries well. This is a good thing: the harvest can be considerable since the St. George's mushroom always appears in groups or fairy rings.

The cap colour ranges from whitish to cream and tanned cream. The cap must be without any regular radial cracks or streaks from the centre to the margins. The cap measures anything between 3cm (1") and 12cm (4¾") — in some cases more.

The gills range from whitish to off-white and do not bruise when cut.

The shape of the cap is ideally dome-like. Older specimens tend to have wavy caps.

The cap must never feature a hump.

The solid, broad stem can be curved (left) but in most cases it is cylindrical (middle) to 'club-footed' (*gambosa*).

The flesh of cap and stem is white and does not bruise when cut. The height of the St George's mushroom is anything between 3cm (1") and 10cm (4"). Note the solid, broad stem.

Positive ID Checklist

The St George's Mushroom

- ☑ Found in group or fairy ring
- ☑ Cap without regular radial cracks or streaks
- ☑ Cap has no hump in the middle
- ☑ Stem solid and broad
- ☑ Gills do not bruise when touched
- ☑ Flesh does not bruise when cut
- ☑ Cap matches cap colour bar (above)

Avg. size across cap:	8cm (3")
Season:	Mainly April to May but can very occasionally be found in summer and autumn
Habitat:	Grass, pastures, woodland margins
Tip:	Always grows in the same place
Culinary rating:	Anything between 0 out of 10 to 10 out of 10

Gambosa means 'club-footed'

The Charcoal Burner

Russula Cyanoxantha

The charcoal burner is a very common and excellent mushroom. Apparently slugs also appreciate its mild flavour which is why tattered specimens seem to be more common than unblemished ones.

The charcoal burner belongs to a group of mushrooms called 'brittle gills' but luckily it has a unique identification feature: its gills are not brittle. They are soft.

Brittle gills

You are looking for a mushroom without brittle gills.

First eliminate the look-alike brittle gills. The gills of brittle gills break off when you move a finger over them and apply pressure. The flesh of all brittle gills is brittle and crumbly.

The essential difference between the charcoal burner and other brittle gills is that the charcoal burner's gills are soft and flexible and feel greasy to the touch. They do not break off when pressure is applied; instead they either resume their original position or stick together.

Note:
With the charcoal burner,
— Gills are white
— Gills are soft
— Gills are greasy to the touch
— Gills do not break under pressure!

The stem of the charcoal burner is smooth and has no ring. It is cylindrical and tapered towards the base. As a rule the stem is pure white but there is sometimes a light, lilac-purplish flush.

The stem is not fibrous and breaks with a distinct 'snap'.

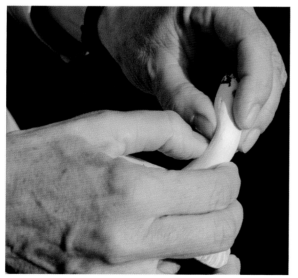

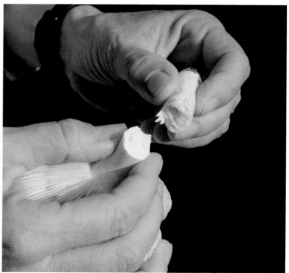

The cap colours vary considerably. There are, however, two main shades: lilac-purple and greenish.

The flesh of the cap is brittle and crumbly.

The skin of the cap can be removed and reveals the lilac-purple-tinged flesh. The stem too is sometimes a slightly lilac-purple colour.

The stem of the charcoal burner, like those of all other brittle gills, is ringless, slightly tapered and has no bulb or sack.

Safe identification begins at the middle-aged stage, fourth from the left, when you can run your finger over the gills. Buttons can't be safely identified.

Positive ID Checklist

The Charcoal Burner

- ✓ Stem cylindrical and tapered
- ✓ Stem has no bulb or sack
- ✓ Stem is ringless
- ✓ Stem breaks with a 'snap'
- ✓ Lilac-purple tinged flesh when cap is peeled
- ✓ White flexible gills
- ✓ Gills do not break under pressure
- ✓ Cap matches one of the cap colour bars

Avg. size across cap:	10cm (4")
Season:	July to October
Habitat:	Coniferous and deciduous woods but mainly beech
Tip:	Always check on the spot for worms ...
Culinary rating:	10 out of 10

Cyanoxantha means 'blue-yellow'

The Amethyst Deceiver

Laccaria amethystina

What a beautiful little mushroom! Although its taste doesn't fully live up to its aesthetic appeal, it is nevertheless a welcome addition to any mixed mushroom dish. It's purple all over and easy to identify, but as with all other species in this book, proceed systematically and tick every box in the ID checklist.

The purple may vary in intensity depending on the degree of humidity. But the mushroom you pick must be clearly and fully purple – despite the whitish fibrous streaks in the stem.

The amethyst deceiver is often found in company with the trumpet chanterelle (see page 140).

Height 1–8cm (½"–3").

Cap size across 1–6cm (½"–2½").

It is equally at home in coniferous and deciduous woods.

The arrangement
of the gills must
look like this.

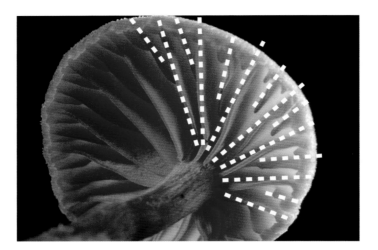

The stem is fibrous
and should be
discarded after
the completed
identification.

After picking
colours fade.
Again: only pick
fully purple
specimens.

Positive ID Checklist

The Amethyst Deceiver

- ✔ Fully purple cap
- ✔ Fully purple gills
- ✔ Fully purple stem
- ✔ Fibrous stem with whitish streaks
- ✔ Gill arrangement as in picture, top of page 84
- ✔ Gills match gill colour bar (above)

Avg. size across cap:	2—5cm (¾"—2")
Season:	August to October
Habitat:	Mainly in deciduous but also in coniferous woods
Tip:	Likes mossy patches
Culinary rating:	6 out of 10

Amethystina means 'amethyst' or 'purple'

The Sheathed Woodtuft

Kuehneromyces mutabilis

This delicious mushroom enjoys universal acclaim. It is excellent in stews: it adds that little extra distinct mushroom flavour which transforms a plain dish into something special. They often grow on tree stumps, hence their nickname 'stumpies'. A good patch might provide more than your basket can take. However, do not harvest indiscriminately! It is of the utmost importance that you inspect each handful carefully and go conscientiously through the ID checklist! You must check on the spot because once cut and handled their the key ID features tend to suffer and become less clear than is desirable.

This is what you are looking for: nice specimens in perfect condition with an obvious 'two-toned' look of cream (centre of cap) and caramel (outer edge) colours.

A battered dried-out patch which doesn't feature much of a 'two-toned' effect.

The sheathed woodtuft grows mainly but not exclusively on deciduous dead wood.

The first step to safe identification is the cap. Take one and crush it between your fingers. If it smells musty, mealy or otherwise off-putting, you're on to something wrong. If it smells nice and mushroomy, proceed with the next steps. The perfect size of the cap for cooking is between 2—5cm (3/4"—2").

The domed caps are nicely wet and glistening. While the hump in the centre dries out to a bright ochre, the margins keep the moisture and appear darker — hence the 'two-toned' effect.

The stem is the key to safe identification. It must feature a ring or residual ring. Above the ring, the stem is bright (yellowish white to light yellow-brown); below it gets darker towards the base. Below the ring, the stem is distinctly scaly.

Stem above ring: yellowish white to light yellow-brown.

Transient ring.

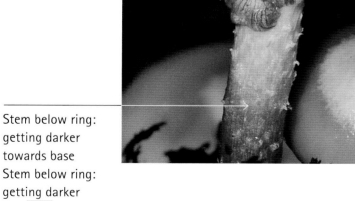

Stem below ring: getting darker towards base
Stem below ring: getting darker and scaly.

Here the ring is almost gone but is still discernible. The scales below the residual ring always remain and must be clearly visible.

A few specimens from the dried-out patch. Although the ID features are still discernible the mushrooms have gone past their best and should therefore not find their way into your kitchen. Note the change of colour and the absence of the 'two-toned' effect.

Only pick the nice wet two-toned specimens as shown in the photographs above.

Positive ID Checklist

The Sheathed Woodtuft

- ✓ No mealy smell
- ✓ Grows in tufts
- ✓ Two-toned cap
- ✓ Stem with ring or remnants of ring
- ✓ Stem above ring: bright
- ✓ Stem below ring: darker towards base
- ✓ Stem below ring: scaly
- ✓ Cap colours match cap colour bar (above)

Avg. size across cap:	3—6cm (1—2½")
Season:	May to December
Habitat:	Mainly on deciduous dead wood (stumps, logs)
Tip:	Always grows in the same place
Culinary rating:	10 out of 10

Mutabilis means 'changeable'

Mushrooms
with tubes

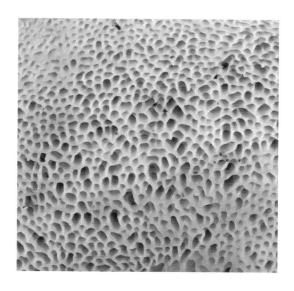

The Cep or Penny Bun Bolete

Boletus edulis

The cep is the king of mushrooms. Some truffles are more rare, more expensive and confined to relatively small areas of the world. The cep, on the other hand, reigns supreme everywhere. Ceps can be found in the same location year after year. They can disappear in certain areas for a couple of years only to return spectacularly in masses. Some people gather only ceps, which is understandable because of their beauty and taste, and the thrill of finding them on the same spot time after time. Ceps vary greatly in general appearance, colour and size. The size of the little fellow in the foreground of the picture above is about 5cm (2")in height whereas the giant is about 35cm (14") in height. If conditions are right (starting off with a wet and humid spring or early summer) you should begin to look for ceps as early as the beginning of July. July and August are the months of the summer ceps.

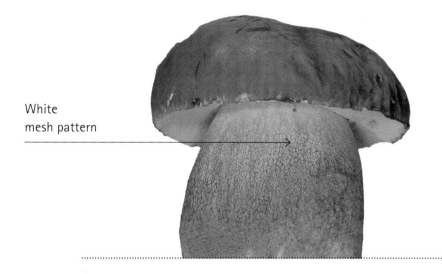

White
mesh pattern

These are summer ceps. All ceps, however, whether summer or autumn, show a fine white mesh pattern on the top of the stem right underneath the tubes.

White
mesh pattern

A classic autumn
cep, the king of
mushrooms.

This is the key ID mark. The white mesh pattern must be visible! All ceps, regardless of their season or stage of development, have a fine white mesh-pattern at the top of their stem.

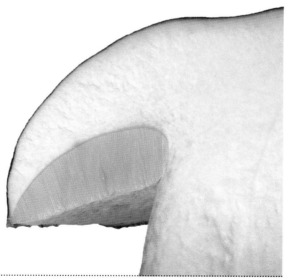

This is what a cep ideally looks like when cut. Not a single worm has even looked at this beauty. Neither the tubes nor the flesh change colour when cut or touched.

Cep tubes are off-white and firm when young. Later they turn yellow-olive and are less firm. In maturity the tubes are olive. Tubes of mature ceps are soft as a sponge and the tubes of old ones are soggy and often like those of the big fellow on page 94. This does not always mean that the inside of old ceps is rotten but, more often than not, this is the case.

Cep stalks vary greatly in appearance. This specimen clearly shows the white mesh pattern all over the stalk.

Nevertheless it is the top section of the stalk just below the cap which matters: a mesh pattern must be clearly visible.

Positive ID Checklist

The Cep or Penny Bun Bolete

- ✓ Tubes, pores and flesh do not change colour when cut or bruised
- ✓ Tubes are off-white, cream, yellow-olive or olive
- ✓ Pores do not show any pink tinge
- ✓ White network on top of stem
- ✓ Cap matches cap colour bar (above)

Avg. size across cap: 13cm (5")
Season: July to October
Habitat: Underneath beech, oak, birch and pine trees
Tip: This mushroom has a lot of stem! It tastes as good as the cap
Culinary rating: 10 out of 10

Edulis means 'edible'.

The Red Cracked Bolete

Boletus chrysenteron

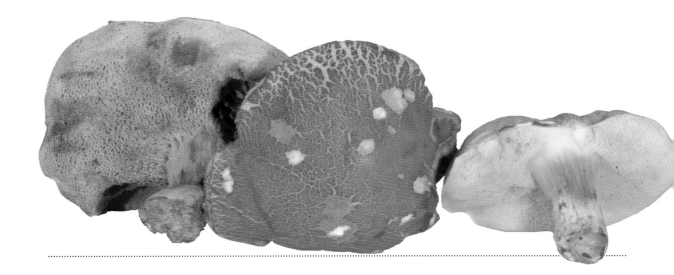

The red cracked bolete is probably the most common of all mushrooms with tubes. Its name describes its key identification feature perfectly. As the mushroom matures, the cracks become more prominent. Opinions on the culinary value differ significantly. The reason is its distinct fruity smell and taste, which divides people. In any case the red cracked bolete should only be picked as long as the pores are bright yellow and firm. The ideal size of the cap is about 2 to 3cm (¾"–1") across. Anything larger will make your dish all slimy.

The colour of the cap ranges from a velvety dark brown to a light brown.

Stems vary in colour. They can be yellow, yellow with a little red or yellow flushed with red.

The stem and pores bruise blue. The intensity of the blueing varies. (See picture opposite page, far left).

This specimen is too old for the kitchen. The pores have lost their brightness. The dull yellow signals that it's no good any more. When the pores are this colour, the mushroom feels soft-to-soggy.

This is the perfect specimen. It has bright, firm golden-yellow pores and a nice firm cap about 3cm (1") across.

The caps are invariably cracked or slightly damaged. The typical identification mark of the red cracked bolete is the red showing through the cracks or the eaten-away patches.

When cut, the white-to-bright-yellow flesh turns blue. This can be very light blue and confined to certain patches.

Positive ID Checklist

The Red Cracked Bolete

- ☑✓ Yellow tubes
- ☑✓ Yellow pores bruise blue (varying intensity)
- ☑✓ Flesh bruises blue (varying intensity)
- ☑✓ Cracks and damaged patches in cap show a distinct red tinge
- ☐✓ Cap matches cap colour bar (above)

Avg. size across cap:	5cm (2")
Season:	June to November
Habitat:	Seems to feel at home everywhere
Tip:	Take only small specimens (i.e. cap no wider than 3cm [1"] across)
Culinary rating:	Anything from 0 and 10 out of 10

Chrysenteron means 'with golden-yellow flesh'.

The Dotted Stemmed Bolete

Boletus luridiformis

I n terms of culinary value the dotted stemmed bolete is on a par with the cep. It appears as early as May and, given favourable conditions, can be found well into November. What's more, there can be bumper years. Cooking the dotted stemmed bolete turns the sauce dark, which doesn't matter. If, however, you want to avoid a dark sauce, blanch the prepared pieces and discard the water.

There is no typical shape for the dotted stemmed bolete.

Likewise the colour of its velvety cap ranges from a leathery brown-yellow to deep dark brown.

The pore colour is light to deep orange-red.

When you think you have found a dotted stemmed bolete, do not cut it open right away. Look at it from the outside first.

The stalk when cut turns blue immediately. The orange-red pores bruise blue. The flesh is yellow.

When cut, the dotted stemmed bolete starts blueing immediately (right). The deep blue fades out after a couple of minutes (far right).

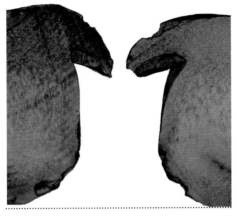

Flesh and tubes instantly turn blue after cutting. Nevertheless there is enough time to see that flesh and tubes are at first yellow before blueing.

Yellow flesh (here not touched by cut).

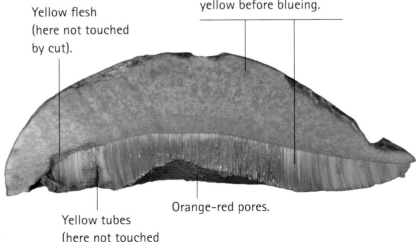

Yellow tubes (here not touched by cut).

Orange-red pores.

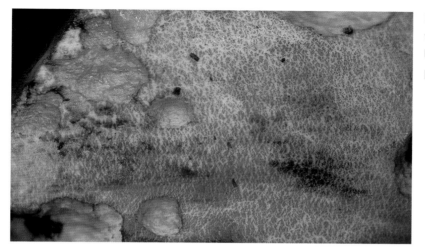

Detail of stem, which also bruises blue. Note the dot pattern.

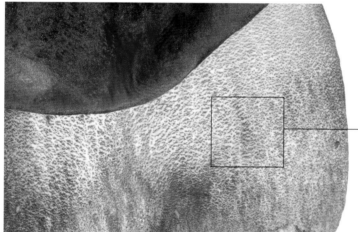

The key identification marks are the red dots on the stem. The dots must be clearly visible.

Dot pattern on stem.

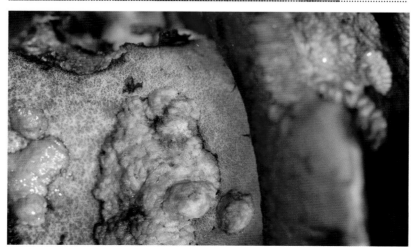

Some dots might have been eaten away. For safe identification, large patches of dots must be clearly visible.

Positive ID Checklist

The Dotted Stemmed Bolete

- ☑ Orange-red pores
- ☑ Pores bruise blue
- ☑ Yellow tubes
- ☑ Tubes bruise blue
- ☑ Yellow flesh
- ☑ Flesh (stalk and cap) instantly turns blue when cut
- ☑ Dotted stem
- ☑ Cap colour matches cap colour bar (above)

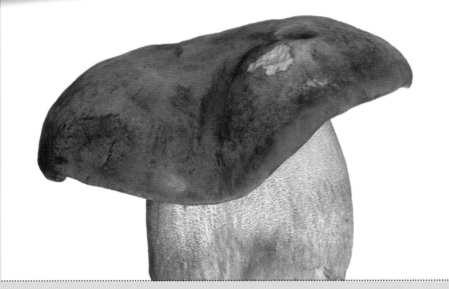

Avg. size across cap:	10cm (4")
Season:	May to October
Habitat:	Seems to feel at home everywhere. Likes acidic soil
Tip:	If you find one you'll almost always find several in the vicinity
Culinary rating:	10 out of 10

Luridiformis means 'of the yellow variety'

110

The Larch Bolete

Suillus grevillei

It is as if pure gold has grown out of the ground — and where there is one nugget, there are others. It's very rare to find a single larch bolete. More often than not, larch boletes form a fairy ring. Always found near larch trees, this beautiful and delicious mushroom is covered with a yellow veil when young (above left). As the maturing mushroom grows, the veil breaks, leaving a transient ring on the stalk (above, centre and right). Always peel the cap of the larch bolete on the spot because otherwise it will make your basket and later your cooking all slimy. In wet conditions, the cap of the larch bolete is always slimy.

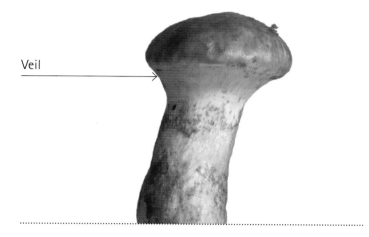

Veil

The veil still covers the cap in a 'baby' larch bolete.

Pick it and check it has tubes (see below).

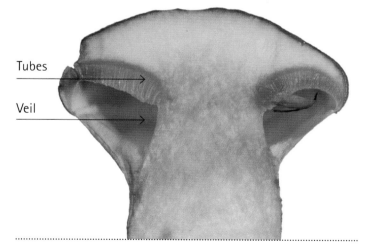

Tubes

Veil

The tubes must be clearly visible when you view a cross-section.

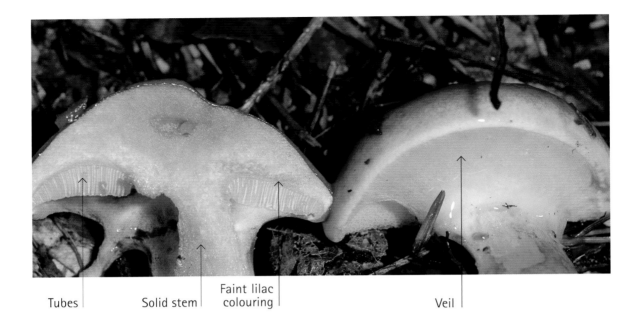

Tubes | Solid stem | Faint lilac colouring | Veil

As the mushroom grows, the veil breaks. This picture (right) shows a larch bolete shortly after the breaking of the veil. The ring is transient (i.e. it often drops off) but even in the mature larch bolete you can always see a mark where the ring has been.

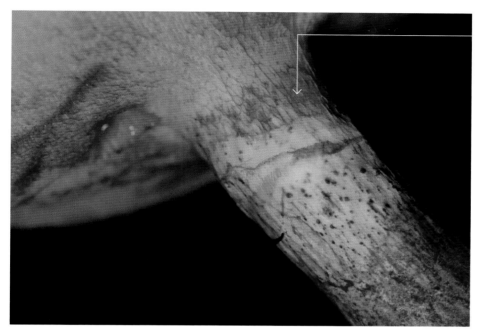

Above the ring marks: net pattern (can be very faint). Below the ring marks: mature specimens show distinct reddish rusty streaks on the yellow stem.

If a larch tree is nearby and you see several gold nuggets, they are bound to be larch boletes. The beautifully golden (and slimy when wet) caps are the key sign. Positive identification, however, requires ticking off all of the identification marks.

Positive ID Checklist

The Larch Bolete

☑ Yellow tubes

☑ Solid stem

☑ Bright orange-yellow or golden-yellow sticky cap (slimy when wet). You have already checked all of the above in the wood

☑ Flesh in cap flushes lilac (faint)

☑ Found near larch trees

☑ Other larch bolete found in the vicinity

☑ Young: tubes covered with a veil

☑ Intermediate stage: ring visible, faint net pattern above ring zone

☑ Mature: ring zone still visible, faint network above ring zone

☑ Cap colour matches cap colour bar (above)

Avg. size across cap:	7cm (2¾")
Season:	June to November
Habitat:	Always near larch
Tip:	Always remove the cap skin
Culinary rating:	9 out of 10

Grevillei refers to the Scottish mycologist R.K. Greville

The Slippery Jack

Suillus luteus

The slippery jack is most often found under the Scots pine but can also grow under other conifers. When wet the cap of the slippery jack is slimy and to some people a bit off-putting. The cap skin is easily removed, however, and what you get is described by some experts as a 'prized' mushroom while others classify it as merely 'edible'. The truth is probably somewhere in the middle.

Although you might find a lone slippery jack, they are usually found in groups near Scots pine or other conifers.

The cap colour is basically chestnut brown (far left). The cap takes on a purplish grey hue (left).

Cap size is from 4 to 15cm (1½"–6"). Always remove cap skin before use – you don't want slime.

Tubes

Veil

The flesh is white to yellowish white, the tubes buttery yellow.

Initially the tubes are covered by a veil which, as the mushroom grows, breaks and leaves a floppy ring.

little brown dots

purplish brown

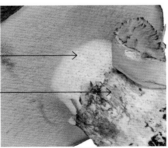

Above the floppy ring, the stem is pale yellow sprinkled with little brown dots. Below the floppy ring, the stem turns purplish brown with age.

Positive ID Checklist

The Slippery Jack

- ✓ Found in groups or fairy ring
- ✓ Buttery yellow tubes
- ✓ Floppy ring
- ✓ Brown dots above floppy ring
- ✓ Cap matches cap colour bar (above)

....

Avg. size across cap:	8cm (3")
Season:	September to October
Habitat:	Coniferous woods
Tip:	Always remove cap skin
Culinary rating:	7.5 out of 10

Luteus means 'saffron' or 'yellow'

The Bay Bolete

Boletus badius

The bay bolete is an excellent mushroom and, by good luck, it is also very common. The main bay bolete months are September and October but it can sometimes be found as early as June. If you find one, there are bound to be others nearby.

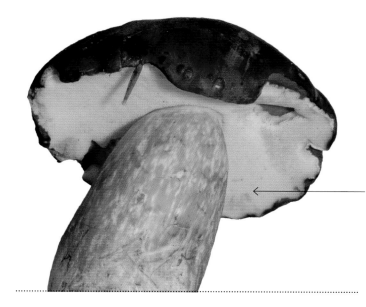

Yellow pores:
This is the stage when the bay bolete is at its best. If the pores turn dirty yellow or green (see opposite page, right) the mushroom is past its culinary best.

The yellow pores bruise green-blue.

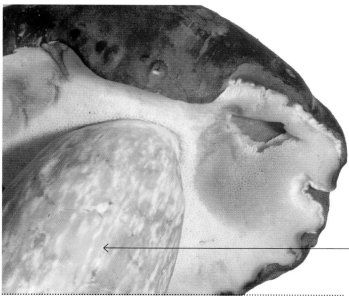

Vertically streaked stem: The background colour of the stalk is yellow-brown and is vertically frosted with brown streaks. The general appearance of the stalk ranges from light to dark brown but the vertical streaks will always be visible.

The young bay bolete has pale yellow tubes which then turn to yellow, olive-yellow and dirty olive-yellow as the mushroom matures. Whatever the stage, the tubes and the flesh bruise blue.

The change in colour of the pores to green-blue when bruised varies in intensity. Here it's quite extreme.

The intensity of the colouring varies but pores, tubes and flesh will always bruise green-blue.

This is what the ideal bay bolete looks like: yellow pores and tubes, white to white-yellow flesh, without a trace of a worm.

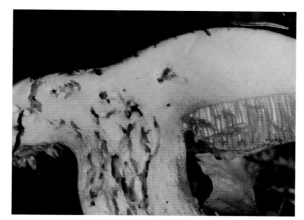

Not as good: but
if you discard the
soft pores and cut
away the wormy
parts, it will still
be excellent.

The colour of the
cap will always
be 'bay' (chestnut
brown)
but bay has a
considerable range.

When wet, the cap will be slightly slimy and this will intensify its colour.

When dry, the colour of the cap will be duller.

Positive ID Checklist

The Bay Bolete

✓ Yellow tubes

✓ Yellow pores bruise green-blue

✓ Tubes and flesh bruise blue

✓ Stem is vertically frosted with brown streaks

✓ There is no mesh pattern of any description on the stem

✓ Cap colour matches cap colour bar (above)

Avg. size across cap:	9cm (3½")
Season:	June to November
Habitat:	Prefers coniferous woods
Tip:	Remove any soft tubes
Culinary rating:	10 out of 10

Badius means 'beautifully brown'

The Birch Bolete

Leccinum scabrum

The birch bolete and its cousin, the orange birch bolete, are the most common of the 'rough stalks'. Rough stalks are mushrooms with a scaly stem. Birch woods or groups of birch trees are the places to look for them. The birch bolete and the orange birch bolete have numerous relatives, all of which have a black or brown scaly stalk. They are all edible but it is recommended to stick to the two species presented here.

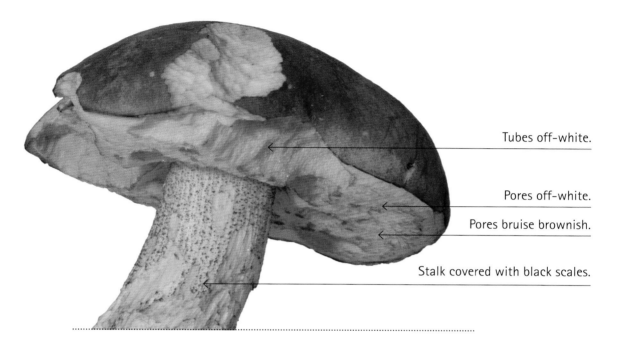

Tubes off-white.

Pores off-white.

Pores bruise brownish.

Stalk covered with black scales.

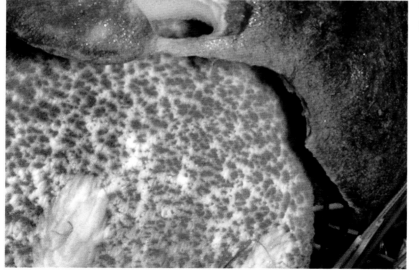

Close-up of stalk, showing black scales.

Pores and tubes change from off-white to a grey-white colour as the mushroom matures. As a rule, you should only pick the birch bolete if it is firm and the pores are off-white.

Occasionally larger specimens are still nice and firm, especially when conditions have been very dry.

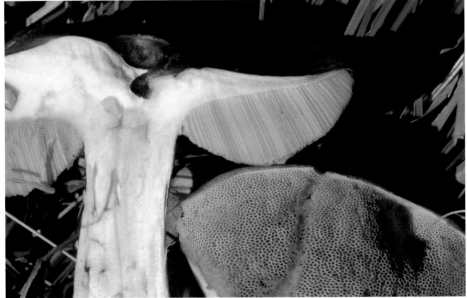

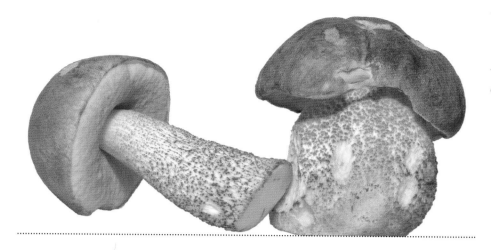

These are the perfect birch boletes: a feast for the eyes and delicious to eat.

The orange birch bolete, *Leccinum versipelle*, is a beautiful mushroom. Its key identification mark is the stem covered with black scales, and of course the orange cap. When cut, the flesh turns faintly blue at the stalk base, displays traces of wine red and finally turns and stays grey. This colour combination doesn't look especially appetizing but be assured, the orange birch bolete is delicious.

Positive ID Checklist

The Birch Bolete

- ☑ Pores off-white
- ☑ Pores bruise brownish
- ☑ Stalk with small black scales
- ☑ Cap colour matches cap colour bar (above)

Avg. size across cap: 9cm (3½")
Season: July to November
Habitat: Birch woods, groups of birch, individual birch
Tip: Discard stem and tubes of larger specimens
Culinary rating: 9 out of 10

Scabrum means 'rough'

Mushrooms with ridges

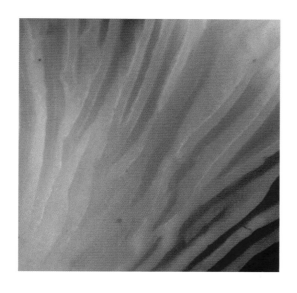

The Chanterelle

Cantharellus cibarius

The chanterelle is not surprisingly a very popular mushroom. It is delicious and very common. Since it is imported throughout the year, the supermarket is a good place to familiarize yourself with the chanterelle. There is, however, nothing like the chanterelle you find yourself. Refrain from picking tiny chanterelles, that is, little yellow buttons which hardly show the identification marks. At some time you'll come across one lonely chanterelle standing there in the middle of nowhere for no particular reason at all. Leave it.

The classic colour of the chanterelle is egg-yolk yellow which, however, can vary from light yellow or yellow-orange to yellow-ochre. The chanterelle does not change colour when bruised. The entire outside of the mushroom is the same colour.

Young chanterelles have a flat cap with a slightly down-curled edge. Do not pick any chanterelles smaller than 3cm (1") high.

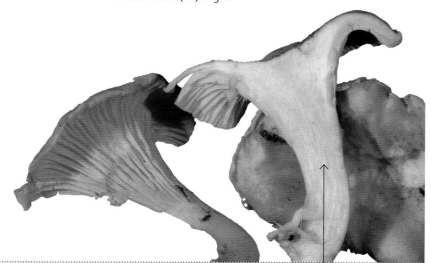

The more mature the chanterelle, the more funnel-shaped it becomes.

The stalk is solid. The whitish to yellowish flesh does not change colour when bruised or cut.

Whether young or mature, the chanterelle's ridges must be clearly visible.

Some mature forms can look highly irregular but, on closer inspection, the funnel shape will still be there.

Positive ID Checklist

The Chanterelle

- ☑ Young specimen: flat cap, slightly down-curled edge
- ☑ Mature specimen: funnel-shaped
- ☑ Solid stem
- ☑ Found in groups
- ☑ Ridges must be clearly visible
- ☑ Colour matches cap colour bar (above)

Avg. size across cap:	5cm (2")
Season:	July to October
Habitat:	In woods with beech, oak, pine and birch
Tip:	Watch for mossy patches with little plant cover
Culinary rating:	10 out of 10

Cibarius means 'belonging to food'

The Trumpet Chanterelle

Cantharellus tubaeformis

In comparison to the attractively-coloured chanterelle, the trumpet chanterelle (also known as the autumn chanterelle, or winter chanterelle) looks modest. On closer inspection, however, it is just as beautiful as the chanterelle. The trumpet chanterelle pops up overnight so quickly that you could watch it grow. It is an endearing mushroom, not least because it tends to appear in great numbers, and is frost-resistant.

A cluster
of trumpet
chanterelles.

The cap is
brownish and
has a depression
(small specimen)
or a hole
connecting
to the hollow stem
in the centre.

Colour and shape
vary according to
age and weather
conditions. Each
individual trumpet
chanterelle has
more than one
colour.

The ridges and the
stalk range from
brown-yellow to
grey-yellow to
grey-lilac.

The jagged edges here are due to frost.

The trumpet chanterelle has a hollow stem.

Conscientiously check each specimen. Can you spot the odd one out here?

Positive ID Checklist

The Trumpet Chanterelle

☑ Found in groups

☑ Brownish cap with depression or hole in centre

☑ Hollow stem

☑ Ridges

☑ Cap colour matches cap colour bar (above)

Avg. size across cap:	2–2.5cm (¾–1")
Season:	September to November
Habitat:	Deciduous and coniferous woods
Tip:	Mossy banks are a favourite habitat
Culinary rating:	9 out 10

Tubaeformis means 'trumpet-shaped'

Mushrooms
with spines

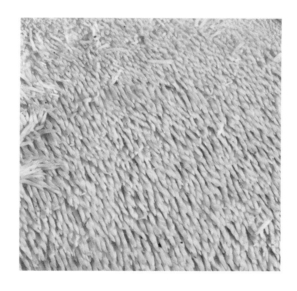

The Hedgehog Fungus

Hydnum repandum

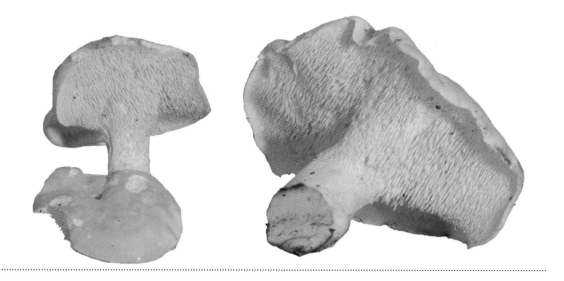

There are other mushrooms with spines but the only one of real culinary interest is the hedgehog fungus. The hedgehog fungus is a great delicacy. It grows on the ground but never on trees.

The spines are the key identification marks of the hedgehog fungus. The flesh is matt white and changes colour in places to a yellow-brown or rusty yellow.

Some hedgehog fungi grow in a very irregular fashion, up to the size of two fists. Nevertheless, all hedgehog fungi have distinctive spines. The specimens here show the entire colour range of the cap. No other mushroom with spines has these colours.

Take only specimens where the spines are clearly visible. The hedgehog fungi pictured here are the perfect size for the kitchen. The cap size is 7–10cm (2¾"–4") across.

Positive ID Checklist

The Hedgehog Fungus

- ☑ Spines clearly visible
- ☑ Flesh matt white when freshly cut
- ☑ In places flesh changes colour to yellow-brown or rusty yellow
- ☑ Found on ground but not on trees
- ☑ Cap colour matches cap colour bar (above)

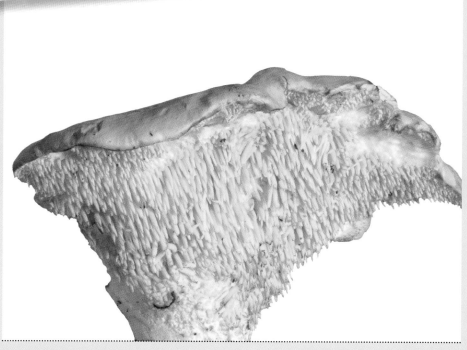

Avg. size across cap:	6cm (2½")
Season:	August to October
Habitat:	Habitat: Coniferous and deciduous woods
Tip:	Avoid older specimens as they can taste slightly bitter
Culinary rating:	10 out of 10

Repandum means 'arching upwards' (refers to the way the cap often reveals its underside)

Mavericks

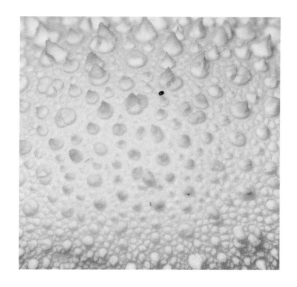

The Morel

Morchella esculenta

M orels open the mushroom season with a fanfare. They might push up as early as February and can be found until May. In certain regions of the continent they are so prized that the details of sites where they are found are left in wills or passed on from the deathbed. They always appear on the same sites. Mycologists distinguish between various species and subspecies of morels. From the identification and culinary point of view this doesn't matter because all morels share the same essential features and are equally delicious. Although you might stumble across morels in your garden, as a rule, deciduous or coniferous woods and railway embankments, sandy soils, meadows and ash trees are your best bet to start your quest for morels.

The morel is one of the hardest mushrooms to find, so study the landscape for clues. The scene above looks distinctly 'morely' because there is a mix of old and young ash trees.

Ash seeds and the characteristic black buds.

Middle-aged ash trees are easily identified by their diamond-patterned bark, which resembles the pitted and ridged structure of the morel.

The bark of young ash trees is smoother but the diamond pattern is discernible.

Top left: Coltsfoot Top right: oxslip and wood anemone.

Left: Marsh marigold Bottom right: Violet.

When these flowers appear, the morel season is in full swing.

The cap is distinctly pitted and ridged. There is no wavy or brain-like shape. The pits and ridges must be clearly discernible, which is when the morel is about 5cm (2") in height.

The form of the cap varies and so do the colours of cap and stem. The colours of the cap range from off-white (when young) to greyish, yellowish brown, brown and blackish brown.

The average size of morels is about 5-10cm (2"–4") in height but they can grow up to 20–25cm (8"–10").

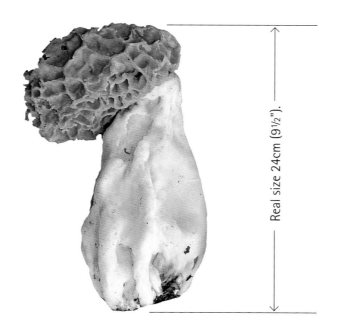

Real size 24cm (9½").

The mushroom on
the left is too small
to identify. It
probably *is* a morel
but the pits and
ridges can't be seen
clearly; therefore
you must give it time
to grow. There is no
doubt about the pits
and ridges on the
mushroom on the
right.

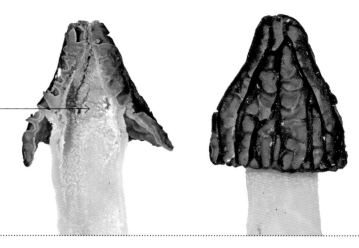

Cap and stem are hollow.

All morels feature:
- Pits and ridges
- Hollow cap and stem
- Symmetry when cut in the middle

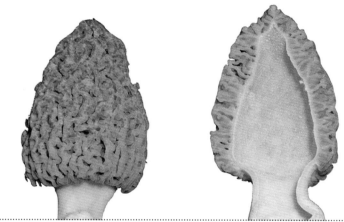

Pits and ridges: these are sometimes also referred to as 'honeycomb pattern' or 'polygonal cavities'.

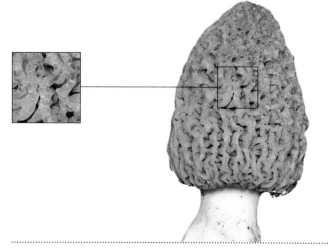

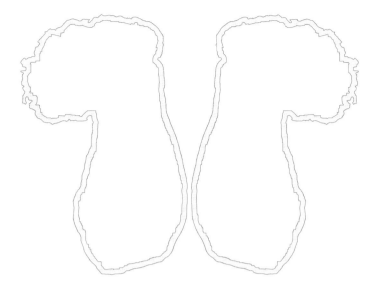

Morels are always
symmetrical when
cut in the middle.

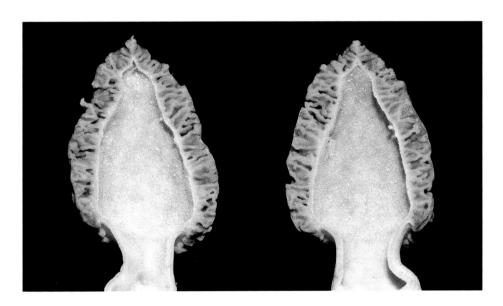

The Morel

- ☑ Appears February to May
- ☑ Cap is pitted and ridged
- ☑ Cap is not wavy or brain-like
- ☑ Completely hollow cap
- ☑ Completely hollow stem
- ☑ Symmetrical when cut through the middle
- ☑ Cap matches cap colour bar (above)

Avg. size of cap height:	3—5cm (1"—2")
Season:	February to May
Habitat:	Meadows, embankments, gardens
Tip:	Tastes best when dried
Culinary rating:	10 out of 10

Esculenta means edible

The Common Puffball

Lycoperdon perlatum

The common puffball is a curious little mushroom. One cluster of common puffballs might number merely four specimens; the next, about forty. The common puffball is a welcome addition to any mix of mushrooms. Cooked on its own, it is not everyone's cup of tea because of its distinctive taste. The giant puffball is another matter and as good a reason as you'll get for a dinner party.

The conical spines are visible to the naked eye and leave an unmistakable mesh pattern when rubbed off. Only pick specimens on which the white conical spines are clearly visible. The common puffball has no unpleasant smell.

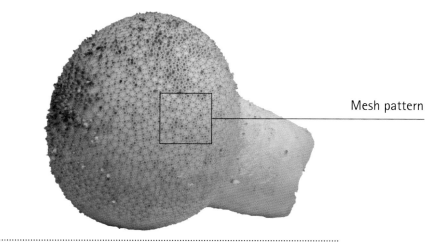

Mesh pattern

These common puffballs are the perfect size (height 3—5cm 1"—2") and condition. When cut, the inside is all white and firm.

Only when the flesh is uniformly white and firm is the mushroom all right to use.

A cousin of the common puffball is the pestle puffball. It too has spines but these are finer than those of the common puffball. It is pestle-shaped and it grows larger (height up to 20cm or 8") than the common puffball. It has no smell. If the flesh is uniformly white and firm, it is good to eat.

The big brother of the common puffball is the giant puffball. Giant means it can grow to one metre (about a yard) in diameter.

From a distance it looks all white but it can have a light yellow or yellow-brown tinge.

The surface is smooth and feels rather like suede. The flesh must be white and firm. Only then is the giant puffball edible.

Positive ID Checklist

The Common Puffball

- ☑ Conical spines
- ☑ Flesh must be all white
- ☑ Flesh must be firm
- ☑ Mesh patterne when spines are rubbed off
- ☑ Colour white to off-white
- ☑ Found in groups
- ☑ No unpleasant smell
- ☑ Cap colour matches cap colour bar (above)

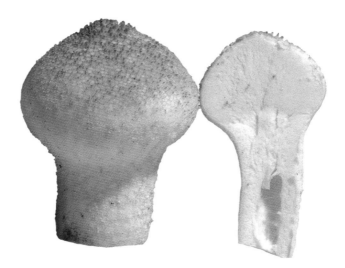

Avg. size across cap:	Size of a golf ball
Season:	July to October
Habitat:	Seems to feel at home everywhere
Tip:	Giant puffballs always grow on the same spot
Culinary rating:	9 out of 10

Perlatum means 'widely-spread'

The Hen of the Woods

Grifola frondosa

For thousands of years, the hen of the woods mushroom has been prized for its medicinal and culinary value in China and Japan. 'Maitake', the Japanese name for the hen of the woods, means 'dancing mushroom', perhaps because those who found a hen of the woods started to dance with joy at discovering such a highly-prized mushroom. The hen of the woods (not to be confused with the chicken of the woods) is a mushroom which can be cultivated commercially. However, the wild hen of the woods mushroom you pick is infinitely superior because, firstly, you found it yourself; and secondly it is as different to the farmed version as is a wild salmon to a farmed one. Finding a hen of the woods is indeed a reason to dance: a culinary event of the first order. And it's good for you too. There aren't many things in life of which that can be said!

The hen of the woods is a cluster of fan-shaped overlapping caps.

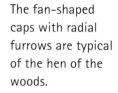

On the underside of the cap the tubes are at this stage (approx. 5cm/2" across) visible to the naked eye. At this point the hen of the woods reaches gourmet status. Start picking now.

Actual size 5cm (2").

The fan-shaped caps with radial furrows are typical of the hen of the woods.

The tubes are clearly visible at this stage.

The cross-section shows a cauliflower-like structure with one central stem. The widest part of this particular specimen is approx. 30cm (12").

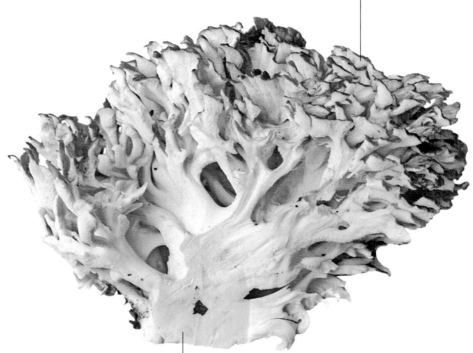

Central stem

On older specimens the tubes are larger in diameter but remain whitish. As the tubes grow larger they almost look like spines — but tubes they are.

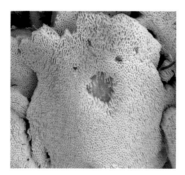

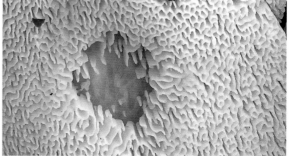

The main colours of the hen of the woods range from off-white, grey-beige, grey-brown, grey-black, brown-black to light brown-black.
The hen of the woods can grow up to 80cm (32") across.

The culinary value of the hen of the woods depends on its age. Some young specimens can grow very big, very fast. These are young specimens: white, firm, fibrous flesh with a pleasant smell. Size is not an indicator of age. Older specimens have a distinct unpleasant odour. Their caps get more and more flabby and the edges crumble.

Positive ID Checklist

The Hen of the Woods

- ✓ Central stem
- ✓ Fan-shaped caps
- ✓ Caps radially furrowed
- ✓ White flesh does not change colour when cut
- ✓ Cauliflower-structured cross-section
- ✓ White tubes
- ✓ Tubes do not change colour when bruised
- ✓ Cap colour matches cap colour bar (above)

Avg. size: 30cm (12") across but can grow up to 80cm (32")
Season: September to October
Habitat: Mainly at the base of oaks but also on other deciduous trees
Tip: Grows on the same spot for many years
Culinary rating: 10 out of 10

Grifola frondosa means 'leafy griffin'

The Horn of Plenty

Craterellus cornucopioides

The horn of plenty is a real challenge to the mushroom forager. Growing low on the forest floor, these mushrooms are so well-camouflaged that you can look at masses of them and not see any at all. If you spot one, there will be more: proceed with the utmost care because they are easily trampled. The horn of plenty is without a shadow of doubt one of the most delicious mushrooms in the world. But it has its price. Cleaning the horn of plenty can be quite a job but the reward is well worth the effort. Besides, when everybody joins the cleaning party, it is fun.

The horn of plenty is a funnel, the outer side of which looks smooth but in fact is slightly wrinkled. The colour on the outer side is ash-grey, grey or pale grey with a bluish or lilac tint.

The inside of the funnel is brown, brown-grey, soot grey or black. The surface is scurfy or flaky and the top edge is curled under. In older specimens the top is wavy and split.

The horn of plenty from above in dry conditions.

The horn of plenty from above in wet conditions.

The funnel shape and the curled-under top are typical.

This looks a rather battered group of horn of plenty. Some of the tops have already split. Don't be put off — they still taste good.

Positive ID Checklist

The Horn of Plenty

☑ Found in groups
☑ Funnel-shaped
☑ Smooth-looking but slightly wrinkled outer funnel
☑ Scurfy inner funnel
☑ Outer funnel matches colour range bar (above)
☑ Inner funnel matches colour bar (below)

Avg. size across cap:	2—2.5cm (¾"—1") across open funnel
Season:	August to November
Habitat:	Near oak and beech
Tip:	When cleaning always split down the middle
Culinary rating:	10 out of 10

Cornucopioides refers to a 'cornucopia' i.e. horn of plenty

The Cauliflower Mushroom

Sparassis crispa

This is the mushroom of superlatives. For many people it is the very best of all. It may be a bit chewy but each bite releases a unique culinary sensation. If you fall for it, you'll be a dedicated cauliflower mushroom hunter for ever. It resembles a cauliflower or a sponge.

Once you learn to recognize its spicy smell, you could identify the cauliflower mushroom blindfold. And then there is the size: it can grow so big that people simply overlook it. This specimen weighed in at 10.2kg (22½lb)

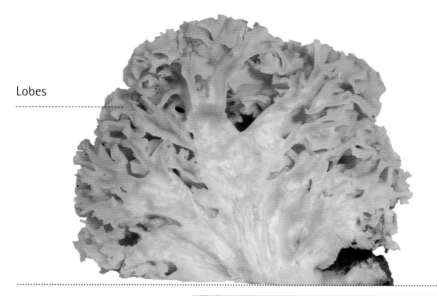

Lobes

Not all specimens grow to giant size. This one here is about the size of two fists. Its cauliflower- or sponge-like appearance and the curved lobes are the key identification marks. There is nothing pointed or jagged in the cauliflower mushroom. The colour ranges from creamy white to light brown. If it turns any browner than the specimen here, it has gone off.

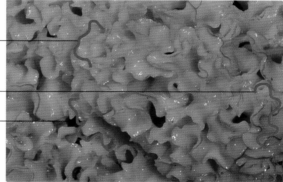

Curved lobes

The Cauliflower Mushroom

- ☑ No gills, pores, tubes or spines
- ☑ No stem
- ☑ Looks like a cauliflower or sponge
- ☑ Lobes
- ☑ Colour matches of colour bar (above)

Avg. size:	30cm (12") across (but can grow up to a metre)
Season:	September to October
Habitat:	Mainly near pine or pine stumps
Tip:	Grows on the same spot for many years
Culinary rating:	10 out of 10

Crispa means 'frizzy'

Trees and mushrooms

Beech, oak, birch, pine, larch and ash are easily identifiable and are excellent pointers to certain mushrooms.

Beech
Especially:
cep, horn of
plenty.

Oak
Especially:
cep.

Birch
Especially:
birch bolete,
orange birch
bolete.

Pine
Especially:
cauliflower
mushroom.

Larch
Especially:
larch bolete.

Ash
Especially:
morel.

Handling, storage and cooking

Cleaning

The first rough cleaning of the mushroom should be done in the woods. Once you're at home, you must verify your mushrooms against the positive ID checklists and then — and only then — can you start the fine-cleaning.

Do not wet mushrooms to clean them. Brush them or wipe them with a cloth. Part of the cleaning process is to check the quality. Evict residents, cut away soft and soggy tubes and cut the remaining mushroom into bite-size pieces.

Basic preparation for fresh or frozen mushrooms

There's a lot of leeway in these basic preparations. The amounts stated can vary considerably and you'll still get an excellent result. And the beauty of it is that you can't overcook mushrooms. The key to culinary success is the quality of the mushrooms.

Serves 4

What you need

Essential: 300—600g fresh or frozen mushrooms
              800ml—1 litre water
              100—200ml dry white wine
              ¾ vegetable stock cube
              1 shallot or small onion, chopped
              100—200ml cream
              10—20g chives or parsley

Optional: A mix of finely chopped vegetables e.g. carrot, courgette
              and celery: approx. 70g
              10—20g chervil

What you do

1. Put water, white wine, vegetable stock and shallot into a pan
2. Do not thaw frozen mushrooms. Add frozen or fresh mushrooms and bring to the boil
3. Reduce heat and simmer until approx $\frac{2}{3}$ of liquid has evaporated
4. Add cream
5. Simmer again until approx. half the liquid has evaporated. Stir occasionally
   If you feel there's too much liquid, simmer until it reduces still further
   The less liquid, the more intense the taste, and vice versa.
   Add water or cream to taste
6. Add salt to taste
7. You now have a wonderful mushroom dish which you can serve with meat (chops, steak, etc.) or on its own with pasta or rice. Sprinkle with chives, parsley or chervil and the finely chopped vegetables

Basic preparation of dried mushrooms

Serves 4

What you need

Essential: 30—60g dried mushrooms
1 litre lukewarm water
1 shallot or small onion, chopped
200ml dry white wine
¾ vegetable stock cube
150—200ml cream
10—20g chives or parsley

Optional: A mix of finely chopped vegetables, e.g. carrot,
courgette and celery: approx. 70g
10—20g chervil

What you do

1. Take the dried mushrooms and put in a bowl or pitcher.
   Add 1 litre of lukewarm water. Soak for 1½ hours (until the
   mushrooms float in brown liquid)
2. Put wine, shallot, vegetable stock, mushrooms and the brown
   liquid into a pan
3. Bring to the boil for 10 seconds
   Reduce heat and simmer until ⅔ of the liquid has evaporated
4. Add the cream
5. Simmer until approx. half the liquid has evaporated.
   Stir occasionally. If there is too much liquid, simmer until further
   reduced. The less liquid, the more intense the flavour, and
   vice versa
   Add water or cream to taste
6. Add salt to taste
7. You now have a wonderful mushroom dish which you can serve
   with meat (chops, steak, etc.) or on its own with pasta or rice.
   Sprinkle with chives, parsley or chervil and the finely chopped
   vegetables

For more about these basic preparations
and on cooking mushrooms, visit the website
www.mushrooming.co.uk

Germs and special cases

Kills all known germs

There is a very low risk of catching something nasty from a mushroom. To reduce that risk to zero, do not eat wild raw mushrooms raw and in the cooking process increase the heat at one stage so that the dish either boils for a couple of seconds or sizzles in the butter. For that brief moment, turn the mushrooms in the pan so that they're exposed to the heat on all sides.

Chanterelle

The chanterelle must not be dried because it goes chewy. It must not be frozen without prior cooking because it will turn bitter.

Horn of Plenty

Some people like it on its own. Others use it only as a spice to add to a mix of mushrooms. In order to find out what you like best, dry and freeze separately.

Cauliflower mushroom

The cauliflower mushroom is also very distinct in taste and perhaps best on its own. Dry or freeze separately.

More on the website:
www.mushrooming.co.uk

Storage

Drying

Drying is the classic way to store mushrooms. This method actually intensifies the taste of the mushrooms and they'll keep for years if you follow the procedure correctly. Do not dry anything you wouldn't eat fresh. Drying cannot improve the overall quality of your mushrooms! There are various methods of drying mushrooms but there is only one way which guarantees consistently high-quality results and that is the only one I recommend: a dehydrator. Whatever the make, the principle is the same: warm air circulation. The sliced mushrooms are placed on trays and then dried in the dehydrator. Dried mushrooms are best stored in any airtight container or a sealed plastic bag and then kept in a dark place. Mix all the species except the cauliflower mushroom. The more species in the mix, the better the taste. The cauliflower mushroom should be dried and stored separately. **Do not dry chanterelles.** All other mushrooms in this book are suitable for drying. Dried mushrooms should be crackle-dry and snap when broken.

More on the website:
www.mushrooming.co.uk

Freezing

Freezing is the other method. I recommend only freezing vacuum-packed mushrooms. Frozen mushrooms retain their colour, texture and taste.

Never thaw frozen mushrooms!
Put frozen mushrooms in sizzling butter or hot water, to retain their texture.

— Mix all the species except the cauliflower mushroom. Again: the more species in a mix, the better.
— I recommend freezing some cep, and horn of plenty, separately. You might want to add just a few of them for a particular dish or use the cep for a tasty starter.

The cauliflower mushroom should always be frozen separately.

The chanterelle must be cooked before freezing. All other mushrooms in this book can be frozen raw.

More on the website:
www.mushrooming.co.uk

Drying or freezing?
Either way, use **only perfectly fresh mushrooms.** Drying mushrooms gives them that deep, strong mushroom taste. The frozen mushroom is more subtle, and the colours of frozen mushrooms are as bright as on the day they were picked, which adds considerably to the pleasure of eating. Dried and frozen mushrooms can be mixed to get the best of both worlds.

More on the website:
www.mushrooming.co.uk

Index